YOUR NEW BABY'S FIRST ADVENTURES

MARTIN BAXENDALE

4

9

14

23

25

29

ALSO BY MARTIN BAXENDALE:

An invaluable and hugely popular in-depth guide to operating, maintaining and servicing a New Baby Unit, guaranteed to ensure many years of trouble-free operation and enjoyment.

→

YOUR NEW BABY

AN OWNER'S MANUAL

MODEL 1001A-GIRL
MODEL 1001B-BOY

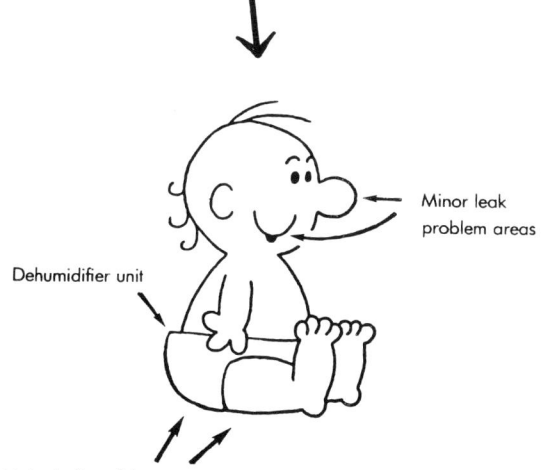

Minor leak problem areas

Dehumidifier unit

Major leak problem areas

"I don't know what I would have done without your wonderful New Baby manual – I had no idea how to work my new Baby properly and thought it might be some kind of novel food-blender until I read your marvellous hand-book." (unsolicited letter from a reader, Mr. A.N. Idiot of Milton Keynes).

WAIL!

Automatic 'Bag-full' signal

(A)

(B)

Fitting your NEW BABY with silencer unit type (A) 'Dummy' or type (B) 'Teething comforter'